# all seeds & blues

# all seeds & blues

Stella Vinitchi Radulescu

Published by CW Books
P.O. Box 541106
Cincinnati, OH 45254-1106

ISBN: 9781936370313
LCCN: 2011924993

Poetry Editor: Kevin Walzer
Business Editor: Lori Jareo

Visit us on the web at www.readcwbooks.com

# Table of Contents

*O Lion,*

> *sing the human song of*
> *tooth and soul, the two*
> *hard things.*

—Paul Celan

*one*
*no, thanks*

# Landing on Holy Silence

If you think it will take
months and years
to start moving and breathing

: *alive*
in the country of blue

music pouring from the ground
a silhouette
ashore in fluid words

the sleepy horse of time...

*

More life coming from the street the child
the scream the squirrel
the language

we invent and Death behind
the house

exotic clothes hang from the trees      stop
walking in my eyes

resurrection
needs no more light for you to land
on holy silence

## The Name

Going round & round the day starts—

      *the blessing*

where

when

whose steps     *letters in the sand*    isn't that
me

my       shadow walking      by the lake


\*

Let's remember

a day a season a street rushed
to the end

the mirror on the wall my face is small
and pale

one wing fell to the ground

the other was taken away    trying to call it

*stillness like blood*
*in the air*

I overspelled my name    Things are like this

they just never seem to be

## This Is the Poem

this is the poem I want to write
in a cubicle form        no rhyme
inside  and with sharp corners a
man on my tongue ready for an
eternal walk   some loose letters
between us          life in a circle

# *just now goldsandaled Dawn*

—Sappho

*just now goldsandaled Dawn:*

the deer came closer to my hand
looking for
flowers

a mother maybe

the sun far west in tears

but this is not really the case     not now

not here

an image in a cage of sounds

nothingness

the grazing
of stars

death by exposure to dreams

## Valse Triste

Stay away from my song     it has thorns

all along it says how I was born and then

reborn       *mental hygiene for humans*

*as they go on*       in winter and how a

whirling tune      thousands of voices

in a big ball     Let's go as far as silence

would take us     kneeling on emptiness

I am not coming back     or I will

the time of saying this :   days and nights

     something wild & mortal

## Mimophilia

wearing your body      let me do it
moonlighting the hills sunbathing the streets
cutting roots with your eyes
trimming the hours

the silky scarf around my neck let me have
your morning dreams
your divinity
I'll pin it in my hair

unbutton my dress I am hungry
I am blue I am not the meaning      your hands
the cold

I have such an appetite for snow

one wing at a time one death

## Less than a Voice

One says it's safe to die to step on the street look at
the clouds
change clothes wash hands pick up the phone talk
to someone

*write what you know* the rule that became so much
an abstraction

no cure for beauty    the point is—
what is the point longer you live shorter the answer
nobody

on the phone
it sounds like voices skipping time went back to
where they belong

# Spring Fugue

Spring came and
storming
the eye the hour
the magnolia
the sun

expandable
beauty
up to my tongue

the goldfinch
the snake
rise
to understanding
hushed
the voice of the past

## The Consulting Room

How is your breathing asked
the doctor and held the stethoscope
close to my heart
I had in mind another thing
a chill an open door    I seldom
act as a rat

Something buzzing over my head
was it enough
I appeared to be red on the screen
a muscle a short figure obsessed
with life sitting

there and nowhere else no breathing
likewise
I looked outside it was silent
and dark and I said
thank you doctor for telling me
that I am dead

## Stone Bed Stone Air

I was neither there
nor here
a storm of years left me
on shore
sleep like milk spilled
who does what in the sick
house
would ever ask
the woman haunted
by her own
heart
stone bed stone air islands
of eyes flowing
backwards
the pillow slips away
her head
a scar that grows
and grows
from the unwanted
flesh

# Judgment Day Music    and Dogs

so go ahead and dump the thing and dumping you get
more
a pair of glasses the Black Sea
or not so black   a sea
like a thought running out of color and salt

one lifetime lease and what's inside the house
I am pretty much done with my life

winter just came
toc toc is someone there with a cane?

If I take the bus to the city
I put on my hat then dump remains and souvenirs
in a vacant lot
dogs are dogs they shit on our graves

it's true and not true if you look the other way
the music
has started

stones would remember a touch a sound—
so much noise in the sky
looking straight in the gaze of stars

who can tell if I am alive

don't hyphenate the heart

## Chamber Music

sunset or dawn
the story starts with a window
cut on low winter sky

interior of an unfinished fruit
the womb
a day between us in love with our shadows

a touch like water     you still here?

lips flowering     black spots
on the wall
the violin dies in a remote spring

orange or the blue dress I would wear

half world

until the last word is said

# What's in the Bag

the lipstick the brush one eye mascara
for clouds
Sappho's *Supreme Sight on the Black Earth*
two dollars to buy rye bread
the pen
Vogue cigarettes
a memo book
God's cell phone

/ marry me flipper
deep water
below /

empty pages mother and father
behind the fence smiling
fading away as I talk
talking
a grave
the golden watch

a gift
from the wedding— stop ticking
you monster
let me alone counting
my treasure
penny by penny
bone
by bone

## No, thanks

Heaven leaks from the inside

the morning light won't fit my window
anymore

the shivering the gold retains
the music

and changes signs

In bold the wind the storm
approaching

no, thanks I won't be you
again

unwanted child

I am feeding the ghost

How many times I told you the good story
the fat story of us

but words don't move along with time

# Dining with Sirens

1.
it was then it is now
time of the day in the spider's eyes
mystic girl in size and sound
the wrestling man takes credit for love

we were so close in black and white
it was then it is now
the hour ready to explode   colors and shadows
break apart

I take small steps in the mirror
a voice enters the room     as a bride
climbs the stairs takes off
the veil

I fall behind
the void
the yesterday of love
what said the Emperor of time

it's not yet known
but humans like to watch the forecast and
to presume life as big and eternal
the receding light

2.
the solitary voice switches

to wind

and wind will grow

in each of us or

take my word the girl I was

relentlessly goes back     it's Spring again—


long after me another season came

but words fall short or maybe death

the woven world     a thread

of years

how does it work

I set the table and flatten the air

like nothing else

or porcelain

## Never Alone

Sometimes is Summer and you shine
sometimes cold

days like home made coffins
you wake up and there is no window to open
no sky

born years ago in the town
of my choice You should remember that and
Would you like to know more Yes

yes but I can't tell what or why a mother came
and said
she couldn't speak or spoke

and spoken is another tense
a coffin made out of hair

and stars
it will be sometime soon

I am never alone or lonely or lone

# The Longest Summer

that violent summer

with no end

ended in words:

time wasn't for living

I am overwhelmed by this lightness

*my fluttering past*

he is my mother my father eventually

my unborn child

an open field     crows
hungry for sweet souvenirs

*Poe on demand*

It is rewarding to live in no time    defiance
good for the climate

I am on my knees

bleaching the lingerie

sanctifying the floor

# Two Inch God Tattoo Etcetera

call me *douce douceur* etcetera

by any means crossing

the silence

mark your Godness

on my skin      black & white

memory stripes


one leg on the road

the trees the smell

the stones—

the other one their absence


somewhere an orphan eye

is looking for you

bastard

unsettling

light

## Open House Streets in the Sky

1.
open house streets in the sky

a crossroads

cars don't stop
late in the week          astronomy

signing papers I got caught in the bureaucracy of stars

a sentence or two tide after tide and so if you cheat

but don't listen—


2.
I still like nights

the logic of the square until the next day

*Harry pushes the button*

go ahead with the rain with your idea of death

talk and talk

the grass will fill up your mouth

## After the Rain

After the rain the Planet is silent
absorbed in deep
meditation

The ocean dozes      tiny ripples
of sleep

A man picks up his cell phone
looks around finds nothing
to say

The beach      a bruised tongue

I brought a pen and a piece of paper
the Earth is clean I can sit on

A wave *as if I need it*
finds its way...

How is to take off your sandals
and step on wet

# From the Point of View of a Rose

1.
what stinks     the volcano it turns out to be a rose

from the point of view

of one word

smoothed by the sea

a rose then *the* rose and the creepers

the wall


2.
euphoria in town—

we left the scene with empty hands

we shouldn't have gone

all the way

to the end

the flight   late   of a single bird

that beautiful Death

# Paysage

Take me to the beach where the air is music
the place for our bodies
to be at large
nights

and days     then more
a minute
a second the full range
of things

Keep me as I am
dozing on warm sand mouth open

you can call me

eternal

\*

The lobster keeps up with his hunger
digging the sea

Dali in the air

Me too
I found the word for *sadness* and the word for *joy*
they are right as I said
happy
in their flesh

More or less

Let me start again

*two*
*all seeds & blues*

## Waiting for the Letter

sky pours then stops

waiting for the letter to come I fell asleep—

green in the air

the metaphor of time rose under weeds and stones

and growing wildly pushed me

adrift

the liquid hour mouth to mouth

love?

the mind needs water from the lake the heart goes
back

to revelation

*We have become enormous*
*just knowing each other*
*with closed eyes.*
—Octavio Paz

## With Closed Eyes

I go by days

and strip by nights

breast bread and naked sky

watch for the womb you know how beautiful I am

pinned down the river like the moon one missing

leg and skipping you ...


The time came closer see the dew the healing on the
other side or

wait a minute

close your eyes

## From a Notebook

divide divide until you hit the whole
thinking of a thought

I start at the bottom
bad things gather in a ditch     Monsieur took his hat

and left the scene
men say hello women take care of the weather

the sky is blue     but Heaven

poets exposed to insanity

## Side by Side

this is a dream you were a child a dream with children
down the road
it's not a dream
I was a child the dust took care of me

as I was dreaming time
went bald

nobody knew the season the hour


\*

whoever dreams and flies knows the unknown I am
looking for bargains
cheap nights a place to stay

we humans and roots rooted in flight
: my turn in you

two words two snowflakes

your death
speaking soft in my mouth

# Orangerie.com

here we go again with the blue
swamped with seaweeds and beauty
the holy splash
long floating
violins

I hear the music I see the sky moving
but touching no
the octopus retracts
am I walking too close

*the show is on*
or maybe too far from when I first saw the flight
Nymphéas on display
I have to stop I have to tie my shoe on the way to
school

the pond
viciously white oh,
how I love the black swan the only one not there

## Ballad for Small Days Becoming Smaller

it's kind of late stores are shut down     where have
you been
the climate changed

like me you missed the equinox
the kettle in the kitchen the whistling    shadows

along the house the balcony
collapsed

heavy words are taking care of us    : desire
music

as we are leaving the town


the phone still rings in the red and yellow decor

## Elegy for the Rain

the train leaves the big eye    the blinking
night in your hair
the cigarette
dying

                                     the rain implores

: nobody comes back    didn't you learn
the rules of ascension
leap

                                     upon landing

on a soft cloth of dreams
the sun is down
his jazzy
bones...

make a wish, man, on your dust

## There Is a Place Called Cemetery

there is a place called cemetery up on the hill
but it's not really that I don't trust
words

: our town where nobody dies

graves still in place
opened for business in a time of peace

closed when the war starts the winter the cold
we have tons of snow

and tons of dirt
in our eyelashes but don't dare to say no

to the rules

little hope first then no hope at all

and we stay in line
waiting for something   one two three
four never arrives

## Chess Playing 1

Before it was said the train departed the lobster
dipped
one leg in the sea
and dead the King came into light


A sudden move the velvet hour teeth and
hunger all in one


Wasting a minute the Fool turns to joy
so does the mouth spread out in all directions if it
happens
it will


Your big green eyes never look at me until the moon
rises

## Chess Playing 2

I don't know the rules I go erratic    to see the sun
I drive East where I left my shoes

under the bed
my raincoat on the chair

a woman keeps telling the story about a piece of land
taken away

Spring came
the heart went the other way


the Queen
has been put to rest the golden casket is filled with
sand

## Chess Playing 3

I play the Queen and you love me and cover my body
with decadent art          the painting
in plain view

those who are blind shiver and those who are deaf
speak

their hunger

Indian Summer chases the seasons          don't think
we are done with the dogwood
blossoms

## Chanson

I drink the sky and play with words
sometimes so drunk
I call you love
take off my dirty clothes
and sleep away
from me
a squirrel tells me Fall is here
I might sit down
and cry
the tunnel
goes and goes no stop between
tracks and stars
the nest is empty I step in    don't know
whose heart
is stepping out

## Spreading Out the News

gardens gardens and all our happy days

the swing hangs loose on the branch     one rotten
rope

the other keeps the illusion

of a rocking world

no children in the air

humans burying humans


caught in a wrong place all eyes—

be kind be merciful November
Night

noises     low sky


the helicopter spreads out the story of us

## All Seeds & Blues

one sound and then another trying to put together
a day—

the red apple

the roundness

one eye and then another help the light
to break in

: you and me we are holding the vase
with no arms

        do not disturb the sleep

all seeds & blues she waits in the shadow her teeth

        as luminous as hunger    one bite
        then another

: somewhere
the snow covered the night

# In Return

I stepped into the day weightless deathless
a sound on the brink

of nowhere

the cracked mouth:

numbers go back to the earth        full ear
in return

from coast to coast seeds and limbs to be called
daughters & sons

stripped to this music

# Redemption

I have built a house on the hill
With little stairs, little hours
Where I am kneeling to worship my death

When evening comes I clean the air
And dust the sun in the yard     night
Eats light    light eats light

A reversible word it's up on my tongue
What I am trying to say it's already said
It's already dust

There is no way to find out
Sounds die in their own flesh as long
As this phrase goes on

We can't split our tongues. My lonely,
Hungry father
Give me again your seed

Seed for a finishing body
My heart like an old city lost in time
Rewords memories     one can see

Leaves on the ground one can hear waves
And strange winds
Eventually get used to the sound

Of your own heart

## The Art

if I could tell how fast is fast

begin the poem with a smile

how cold is cold

whose turn this turn

if I could tell what is the mind

besides this glow from bone

to bone

if night already came

or comes

if time means time and nothing else

the skin, the man—

if Nothing could come close

and closer

if

*Stella Vinitchi Radulescu*

# Let's Talk Molloy the Joyful Return

*For at first sight the heavens seemed uniformly gloomy.*
—Samuel Beckett, *Molloy*

let's talk Molloy the joyful return the old face
of Earth

voices hailed from inside and the hill
of nowhere

I mean the red hill and spitting out a mother
from womb

*a story to tell*      vitamins for the brain
I can count on progress

on Dali's paintings and lighten my face
with a match

or matching
a hog a Hindu temple several ideas several gods

I continue to take notes

you never know      the small side of things
or you know or you don't care

neither

you nor me

and I am saying this

## Ballets Russes

Have you ever seen a ghost
the trembling of the house / space moving ahead

shape of a skull

beauty in its final stage

: trophy down
because it's the end of the war

small feet on the ground tulips
and daffodils
the trot

trottiner trottinant
the pavement of death


\*

Nijinski in red
let's bury him in his own flesh
face up
solid all across

from right to left *glissando*

wet wet floor

we were children in a remote time
mothers like angels
flying around

*Peace on Earth* nothing to talk about:

people in our town—
they are still building bridges of blood

# Retreat

in one sound

enough space to build

your summer

house

briefing your life

late evening

under

the stars

enough time

to catch the last

flight—

*Tristia* said the poet

and then

he died

## Ars Poetica

voices from the heat of the night
targeting my lips

clouds dispersed
            the moon declining


playing deaf in the era to come you bought crutches
props

icy gloves


            I bought an extra leg and stood in the wind

            oceanlike silence

            blueness of raw sounds


: let me go unseen and unloved a corpse in its way to
transparency

## September Sun

*This is the final day of years of sweetness.*
—Petrarch

when we planted the oak
it was September
Spring in Brazil
Winter
under our feet
nineteen days after the making
of the planet
no time that I know
took roots
in her grave sleeping
face down
not to see not to be touched
a sigh came out of
the ground
shoveling worms
dirt
the tapering light
winds split us
this blood on our hands
branches
and leaves
in numerous parts
this September sun

## History at a Glance

I knew him     a hat
and a silk tie

freedom under the skin

shining ahead
eyes looking at me while everything else falls

from view

he left the house and we start eating and shopping
December in town

I was supposed to wear old clothes black shoes and
walk

to the end

Winter blue freezing hands     hands that couldn't
match a prayer


People from the nearby town are sending us historical
letters

## Ballets Russes 2

1.
Flesh and less flesh water and clouds

Don't close your eyes
This is the time to watch the ballerina

To believe in angels their sweat their complexion

The natural gleam

What we should know / fire and ash


2.
It goes like this up and down Heaven and Hell

                Or imagine you—

Try to put one foot on the Earth

                last move

Cradle us and remember the flood

                what remains after us

# The Language Shrinks on Its Way

onion soup and the death of a child
have in common
the timing
five o'clock news      it snows—
it snows in one place
the brain keeps snowing
everywhere

whose coat am I wearing
a metaphor for tree
or crypt
various things linked by color
and sound
turquoise they highlight
the route

as the signs disappear
where to go now the world
is not an option      the old
refrain
empty      empty
and what to do with my hands
almost no hands

as I talk to you

## Dante's Momentum

*"...l'amor che move il sole e l'altre stelle."*
　　　　　　　　　　　　　　—Dante

You gave me the name of a star
but I feel earth in my mouth not fire
a spark

this wrong beauty of ours

Dante's momentum is already gone　　blue
in the flesh

the pond in its autumn glow:

Only one name returns
when I look down—

It slowly moves the sky

## From Where We Stand

from where we stand     let's say the valley—
saliva rises
we should talk     talk sunset and talk butterflies
fire on top of the pines
hills sinking
in sound
up to the throat the wolf the illusion hysterical
clouds
slightly left looking from inside somebody
*a woman*
waves to us and we could almost be there
lay on the ground word after word
listen to the echo

deepen the time

*three*

*zone*


*Adieu   Adieu*

*Soleil cou coupé*

—Apollinaire

## Complicity

in front of the window the big tree fell down
cars stop at no sign
little by little

the notebook eats my shadow I see the crack
disappearance of one finger
then two

I play the ghost I feed you     bread and wine
sand and snow:

up to your name I have to climb
this Everest of light

## The Waste as It Comes

a bad day deserves a bad body a bad body
deserves no soft words
no warm water to wash away the dirt the waste
as it comes with the sun in small portions
of life

the skin like an old fabric keeps creasing
and crushing look around
look underneath you'll be surprised to see
how many planets are dying to make a day
like this

# A Family: the Metaphor

I opened the wound and looked inside:
so many years of cozy
afternoons

a floating house

I must have been awake and slim
four by four the time of being
a family:

the metaphor
oh, yes, the youngest broke the silence

the oldest still longing for me
names were written roads were cut

a paragraph missing       first letter still hangs

from the tree

## Diving with the Whales

the pilot whale like the pilot light keeps our sea from
retracting

wide open the shell of time

I keep talking talking cut my way through the waves

the whale joins me      white for the teeth

crimson for remembrance


stars browsing through the lost pages

## Starting Point

1.
at the beginning of the light
the clock was set up to this very moment
a road was cut

life didn't happen for centuries
then my parents came and gave me flesh

here I am      a heart made out of frozen seconds
a second itself freezing in front of your eyes

this is what makes this moment alive
my body to grow
to seek understanding


2.
and what if I fail and what if I don't
the day is not what you see the apple is not
what you want

desire keeps dripping around

this is how it is, the big lie which makes us feel
good
about our selves

forgive me for talking in no voice
for not bleeding peacefully like the sun

3.
the answer is in our hands
but we don't understand      a long time ago

we named things at random
now we are paying for it

we don't see a soul like we see the moon rising
we don't understand simple facts

where are we going
why do the seagulls cry      I have these words
sometimes I feel like touching their flesh
the roundness
and then I let them fall
one by one into your mouth, Mr. Nothing

make me an offer
I will buy your big and burning eyes


4.
now is the moment for the tide to rise for you to be
here
to ask and to cry
to be young to be old      to check the weather
to bury your friend

now is the moment to make your bed
go to sleep

doucement doucement
falling into a long dream

\*

mirror of clouds
no earth no whispers
no hidden meaning under the shrine
nothing about snow
about us gripping the dark

we have learned the music

a second lit in our palms

# Purple

I have a purple face you see
the damage of the purple wind I was playing with
one summer
in a remote town

it was a shortage of hot water and colors
your ID, said the man he looked at me
and put a purple stamp on my face

it went inside like a tattoo ran down my veins:
puddles of silence small streams of time

it's somehow the color of being alone

\*


To be chaotic to be exotic to be erotic     small needs
from big sounds
the urgency of a purple word on my tongue

I believe in you as a mirror
I believe in long nights short days

cover me with your breath, your purple disbelief
I am not from here and I feel the pain

my heart unfolds its daily song
as if I were happy

## The Gate Was Open

the gate was open but my hands were cut

late afternoon

we are having a party

some were asleep some not

some throwing bombs out from the roof

who you

the sleepers watching from their sleep

I was looking for you

forgot the language

a funny noise under the oak, Mother?

despair and joy:    have the feeling


one says that cut off from the world the body

still keeps breathing

## Zone

and then she cried cries would cry
will cry   verb after verb
for the boy yesterday so little
in her arms

for not being able to reach and hold him again
for not being able to hold
the woman she was

in the garden

or the garden itself

wrinkle after wrinkle the earth cracked
her face blew up
and the night
threw his heavy coat over the house—
brightness

always fades away
vowels turn into broken consonants
this is
what
I remember

unless
something was real   like the flesh
in its absence:
rush
rush to see me : the statue

is already in your eyes

# Ritardando

first it was the hair like a black pumpkin
on top of the head then the man the trumpet

: drops of rain

a wheel-chair speeding the afternoon light and
the noise
in my chest

\*


beachseagullshoneysuckle and all...

a cavity

the engine hum & hum the wind doesn't stop either
a thought ahead I almost lost balance two boys
bicycling
they let me pass it's like a bridge

a bridge in the air I have to rush      colors
slip out of the eye

the neighborhood has changed, my dear, boys
have put
away their bikes

the sky is beneath you

the sea left

\*

as if I was trying to come back

as if I had slept a thousand years

# Moonlight Sonata

Sweet comes from ashes: bones
in the sweetness of sleep,
diffusion of dreams. Adjectives
picking up from the ground a color, a sound.

Summer on the kitchen floor makes dirty waves,
the boy
next door still practicing the moonlight sonata.
He gets stuck there, always there, the long arpeggio
where the wind reaches the linden trees.

We are on our way to salvation, we definitely have
blue hair, eyes as many as birds—
meet the monster licking the hour from the plate.
He wants to smash it, the immensity.

I have the power to say no, I have a body that fits
tragedy,
when I am green I sink in the Atlantic,
yellow makes me look like a snake.
No heaven, no metaphor.

First I was a voice, then a flame, then the idea of
flame,
the ghost. If by any chance I am God,
I'll take the night for granted
and sleep on the coach.

# Rilke Died

Rilke died, the world goes on.
Black roses falling
On the roof.

One angel at a time.

I see a monster rising
In my child's eye,
Flesh and air in a glance of light.

The ocean waves its back,
Love on top, like foam.

## So Much Night

so much night between leaves
between roses and daffodils between hands holding
roses and daffodils
between stars holding the garden

I am on the other side of the fence seeding snow
at the root of the nights

## New Look the Corpse

The crazy man is not crazy enough, he thinks he is
alive.
His neighbors buried him when it was the case. The
sun came
        down.

Children were watching. I was watching, you maybe
were
        watching too.

*Oh, honey*
I said, *death fits you well.*

Between squalls of Northern wind he smiles and
moves his
        feet.

Not dead enough, walks on the street, takes the bus.
Still has to pay the rent.

Life gets more expensive every day.

New look the corpse between leaves and twigs.

What goes around ends in a ditch.

## White on White

what I wouldn't like to call or hang on the wall
a woman with a square face

getting darker while I am saying this

that night in my throat     all the dead stars


\*


there are many options, first word beside the void
at the door—

a little beast owns the floor

a look without eyes
white on white

piece of silence covers the snow

## *Le Déjeuner sur l'herbe*

after Edouard Manet


We sit in the sun with white plates in our hands.

Far away a tune fades in the air.

Our lives go by.

\*


At sundown my mother bakes the bread: flour, salt,
water.
With her fingers she works the dough, makes a little
hole,
sets the yeast in the middle.

Later on milk from the moon     her grave shines by
the river—
children unborn little dark tongues
milk on the kitchen floor

o, mother

night up to the end,
country of all forgiveness

## Day After Day

the pillow sits on the bed my hair grows green
water runs from the celestial faucet
I soap I wash my dreams

four windows are black the rest are waiting for you
your view of this place
every hour the same

as four or twelve
the train I have to take or I have taken
still between tracks

sometimes I don't wake up
sometimes I do and make a tea in a white cup
the wind keeps haunting my blue house

colors leek from above I pick up the phone
too far the end of the line
I swallow the air

take my coat my umbrella go nowhere

# At the Station

### 1
The railroad was white with heavy snow.
My father stood still in a wooden frame,
Russian, buttoned tunic, my mother wore a black
Dress for the ball.


Was it yesterday or today? Was it during the flood
Or during the war?
Was I too little to know I was alive?

*Then I could fly like a kite, lie down on the kitchen floor,*
*The smell of the stars in my hair, I could separate seasons*
*By looking in my mother's eyes.*


### 2
The railroad ended in a small station, men and
women
Took their bags, crossed the tracks.

*Time stops here,* announced the loud-speaker,
My parents were smiling in an awkward way.
I touched them, I waved.
The picture someone took is all blurred.

Time for the heart to take over whatever remains.

## Last Call

I called home. The phone rang.
Far away a man stands still at the door.

*I am calling from the station, mother?*

The voice makes loops, circles the streets,
plunges inside:
empty house, echoes of small animals running
the floor.

The last train was leaving.

Now. They are pouring wine and boiling wheat.

They sing, make strange noises.

The phone rings. I rush to answer, someone pushes
me away.

A candle, the old carpet.
Green and red birds are filling the sky.
I am at the station. *Hello?*

Corpses last, they don't talk.

## Chicago Etcetera

I left at nine, it was too crowded.
I left my glass   pinot grigio   on the table.
I couldn't light my cigarette.
I was sweating.

Look at the sky, you stranger, you don't have any
eyes.

I shut the door.
A shadow behind me, a small animal.
I wanted to be a swan.
I thought how nice to think of a swan.
In a night like this.
No stars.

I looked for my keys.
Do I really have a heart ? In fact,
no facts, unless I close the window
to avoid suicide.

## Night, as Always

And yes, I will tell the truth
And pour more wine.

Nothing hurts more than two empty glasses.

Night, as always.

The street.

People running up and down
Looking straight in the middle of nowhere.
Disappearing.

Between us layers of time
Like skin

Music that will not last. Someone already
Died in our eyes.

## Not as Beautiful

I am not as beautiful as you think I
am not as blue as you dream when you
open your eyes

I stand still hooked on your hunger the moon
reaches me
my hair my arms I

look in the mirror
I grow more and more beautiful

in your mind—
you are tearing apart the whole universe

close your eyes let me alive

## In Static Waters

Last move
what to expect     the dome of hours floats
away

there is a feeling about

[ . . . . . . . .]

Next

the broken line     the snake

wakes up to see

the bruise


*

Springtime again and we are due
for love

in static waters there is a sign that slowly moves
to knowledge     oppressive as the sky

could be
it promises relief    what we can grasp

a word or two
on ever

dying
lips

## Black Curtains

Black curtains. The curtains are black.

I have never seen the light. May I call it a chair,
a red chair by the sea, the immaculate pig—
*tristesse du soir sur le balcon*

the balcony with a small view:
Earth growing old and older and oldest.

A window opens.
People I know from the other life
are pumping beauty on the grass

and sleep in golden veins of time.
What happened to my body? I was wearing
my daily gown half-flame

half-shadow.  It's not my time,
white snake,
take it from me and put it back in the trees.

## Acknowledgments

*Rhino*                        All Seeds & Blues

*Laurel Review*                There Is a Place Called Cemetery
                               Let's Talk Molloy the Joyful Return
                               The Consulting Room

*Chiron Review*                Elegy for the Rain
                               Less than a Voice
                               Judgment Day Music   and Dogs

*Karamu*                       From Where We Stand
                               Chanson

*Visions International*        This Is the Poem
                               Night as Always

*Tupelo Press Poetry Project*  September Sun

*Asheville Poetry Review*      Mimophilia

*Spoon River Poetry Review*    The Name

Some of these poems appeared in the two chapbooks, *Last Call* (2005) and *Diving With the Whales* (2008) published by March Street Press.

I want to express my sincerest gratitude to David Dodd Lee for his invaluable editorial assistance and untiring support of this work.

## About the Author

Stella Vinitchi Radulescu, Ph.D. in French Language & Literature, is the author of several collections of poetry published in the United States, Romania and France, including *My Dream Has Red Fingers* (2000), *Last Call* (2005), *Diving With the Whales* (2008), *Insomnia in Flowers* (2008).

A recent nominee for the Pushcart Prize, she is the winner of two International Poetry Prizes, awarded for her books published in France, *Terre Interrompue* (2007) and *Un cri dans la neige* (Editions du Cygne, Paris, 2009).

She has had poems in *Seneca Review, Pleiades, Karamu, Louisville Review, Rhino, Laurel Review, California Quarterly, Visions,* among other magazines, as well as in a variety of poetry reviews in France, Belgium, Quebec and Romania.

CPSIA information can be obtained at www.ICGtesting.com

233986LV00001B/49/P